Zoom in on HONESTY

Rita Santos

Enslow Publishing
101 W. 23rd Street
Suite 240
New York, NY 10011
USA

enslow.com

WORDS TO KNOW

citizen A member of a nation or community.

civic virtue A behavior or habit that is good for the whole community.

consequence The result of a choice or behavior.

dishonesty Saying or doing things that are not truthful.

honesty Speaking and acting in a way that is truthful.

journalist A person who researches and reports the news.

legend A story that has been told for many years. It is often not completely true.

moral Good and right.

tax Money that is paid to the government to help pay for public services.

trustworthy Able to be trusted.

CONTENTS

Speaking honestly with others helps us gain their trust and respect.

What Is Honesty?

Honesty is when we tell the truth. When you are honest it makes people feel good because they trust what you say and do. Being honest is helpful because it means everyone has the same information and can make good choices. Honesty also is a sign of respect. It shows you value the other person enough not to lie.

Civic Virtues

Honesty is a civic virtue. "Civic" means having to do with the community. A virtue is an idea or behavior that is considered good and moral. So a civic virtue means that the citizens of a community behave in a way that is good for the whole group.

Every place we go has rules for what you can and can't do there. You can yell and shout in the park, but in the library you must speak quietly. When you go to school you know that the teacher expects everyone to sit at their desk when class starts. This behavior helps the class run smoothly. Civic virtues help tell us the rules of our communities.

Raising your hand before speaking is a common rule in the school community.

Words and Actions

When we talk, we know that being honest means not telling lies. But we can be dishonest with our actions, too. Sometimes you might not be sure if your actions are dishonest. If you feel like you have to hide what you're doing, it's probably dishonest. Doing something you've been told not to do, even if you don't get caught, is still dishonest. Honesty makes our communities better because people know they can trust each other.

Honest George

One **legend** about George Washington, the first American president, is that he could not tell a lie.

When to Be Honest

It's easy to say we should always be honest. But being honest isn't always easy. Sometimes it can be scary to tell the truth, especially if you think someone might get in trouble if you do. Our friends might even ask us to lie if they are afraid of getting in trouble. It's okay to want to help your friend, but lies make problems worse, not better. A friend who asks you to lie needs help. The only way to help him is to tell the truth.

Sometimes we are scared to tell the truth because we are afraid we might get in trouble.

The Boy Who Cried Wolf

We should be honest in all parts of our lives. Being honest is how we earn the trust of our families and community. Dishonesty hurts people. You've probably heard the story of the boy who cried wolf. He lied so often about what he saw that no one believed him when he really did see a wolf. This put his community in danger. If the boy had earned the trust of his community, he would have been able to protect them from the wolf.

Trust Me
People who are known for being honest are called trustworthy.

Honesty in the Community

Honesty is an important civic virtue for many jobs in our community. Politicians are chosen based on what they say they will do for the community. Citizens trust politicians to honestly represent the views of everyone in the community. Lying has consequences. When politicians are dishonest, many citizens choose not to vote for them again. A politician who keeps his promises earns the trust of his community.

It is important that politicians speak and act honestly since they represent all of the people in their community.

Being Honest at Home and at School

It's important to be honest wherever we go, even at home! What does honesty look like at home? Imagine that your parents go out for the night and leave you with a babysitter. You might be tempted to tell her that you're allowed to stay up late. This would be dishonest. You want your babysitter to trust you in case there is an emergency. Also, if your parents come home early you will both get in trouble!

It is important to be honest with babysitters and other caregivers. They must be able to trust you in order to take good care of you.

Think Before You Speak

Being honest is not an excuse to be mean. Saying something that is true but hurtful is not nice. If you tell your sister her new haircut is ugly, she will be sad. You may have said something you think is true, but it still hurt your sister's feelings. Sometimes it is better to keep your thoughts to yourself, even if you believe that they are true.

False Claims

Plagiarism is when you claim to have written something someone else wrote.

Cheaters Never Win

Tests in school can be really hard. Everyone wants to get good grades. If you don't know the answers, you might be tempted to cheat. That would be dishonest. Even

Cheating is never a good idea. You won't learn anything, and you may get caught!

though you don't want to disappoint your parents with a bad grade, they would be more disappointed if you cheated. It is better to try your best and fail than to succeed by cheating.

Being an Honest Citizen

It's important to be a good citizen! Every year the government collects taxes. The government uses the money to build roads, schools, and parks. Some citizens lie about how much they owe in taxes. This hurts the community because there is less money to pay people like teachers and police officers. Honest citizens do not lie about their taxes. Honest citizens pay their full share of taxes. Being an honest citizen helps make our communities nicer to for everyone to live in.

Paying taxes can be painful, but it is important to the community that all people pay their fair share.

Following the Laws

In many places, it's against the law to drive without a seat belt. Good citizens remember to wear their seat belts even though no one would know if they didn't. Not wearing a seat belt is against the law. It's also selfish and dangerous. Imagine how many people would be upset if you were hurt in an accident. Honest citizens follow laws that keep themselves and others safe.

Buckle up! Using a seat belt is an important rule for every citizen.

19

Journalists must do their best to tell people the truth.

Reporting the News Honestly

It is a journalist's job to accurately and honestly report the news. Journalists do research and talk to many people when they are reporting on a story. They want to make sure they don't miss any important information. But be careful: not every piece of news you read is truthful.

The internet is a great place to find news articles, but you shouldn't trust everything you read online. When you read news online you should ask yourself who wrote the article and what point they were trying to make. When several journalists from different news groups agree on the facts, it's a good sign that the information is probably correct. Lots of people like to share news articles over social media. Keeping each other informed is a good thing, but as citizens we must be sure only to share articles we know are true.

Tell the Truth

Honest citizens make our communities happy and safer places to live. If you want your neighbors to be honest, you must be honest too! Respectful communities value honesty as a civic virtue. We should be honest when we're at home, at school, and everywhere! Life is better when we trust each other. Being honest is easy! Just tell the truth.

ACTIVITY: IS IT TRUE?

How much of the news is reported honestly? Let's find out!

1. Choose an article from your local newspaper. Use the internet to find three other articles about the same subject.

2. Compare each article. What information appears in each article? What information is left out of other articles?

3. After reading all four articles, what do you think really happened?

4. Do you trust the information in all of the articles? Write a paragraph explaining why or why not.

LEARN MORE

Books

Ashdown, Rebecca. *The Whopper*. Sommerville, MA: Templar, 2015.

Cook, Julia. *Lying Up a Storm*. Chattanooga, TN: National Center for Youth Issues, 2015.

Sommer, Carl. *The Boy Who Cried Wolf*. Houston, TX: Advance Publishing, 2014.

Websites

The Constitution for Kids

Usconstitution.net/constkidsK.html

Learn the history of the United States Constitution and Bill of Rights.

George Washington and the Cherry Tree

www.history-for-kids.com/george-washington.html

Read a fun poem about young George, who could not tell a lie.

INDEX

Published in 2019 by Enslow Publishing, LLC.
101 W. 23rd Street, Suite 240, New York, NY 10011

Copyright © 2019 by Enslow Publishing, LLC.
All rights reserved.

No part of this book may be reproduced by any means without the written permission of the publisher.

Library of Congress Cataloging-in-Publication Data
Names: Santos, Rita, author.
Title: Zoom in on honesty / Rita Santos.
Description: New York, NY : Enslow Publishing, 2019. | Series: Zoom in on civic virtues | Includes bibliographical references and index. | Audience: Grades K-4.
Identifiers: LCCN 2017046443| ISBN 9780766097711 (library bound) | ISBN 9780766097728 (pbk.) | ISBN 9780766097735 (6 pack)
Subjects: LCSH: Honesty—Juvenile literature. | Conduct of life—Juvenile literature. | Citizenship—Juvenile literature.
Classification: LCC BJ1533.H7 S255 2019 | DDC 179/.9—dc23
LC record available at https://lccn.loc.gov/2017046443

Printed in the United States of America

To Our Readers: We have done our best to make sure all website addresses in this book were active and appropriate when we went to press. However, the author and the publisher have no control over and assume no liability for the material available on those websites or on any websites they may link to. Any comments or suggestions can be sent by e-mail to customerservice@enslow.com.

Photo Credits: Cover, p. 1 © iStockphoto.com/Figure8Photos; p. 4 Stock Rocket/Shutterstock.com; p. 7 Syda Productions/Shutterstock.com; p. 10 George Rudy/Shutterstock.com; p. 12 Pressmaster/Shutterstock.com; p. 14 Photographee.eu/Shutterstock.com; p. 16 racorn/Shutterstock.com; p. 18 WAYHOME studio/Shutterstock.com; p. 19 Syda Productions/Shutterstock.com; p. 20 2p2play/Shutterstock.com; p. 23 Pavel L Photo and Video/Shutterstock.com; illustrated hands pp. 2, 3, 22 back cover gst/Shutterstock.com; illustrated child with ball pp. 5, 9, 13, 17 gintas77/Shutterstock.com.